Introducing Exmoor

TREVOR & ENDYMION BEER

Bossiney Books · Launceston

First published 1999 by Bossiney Books
Langore, Launceston, Cornwall PL15 8LD
© 1999 Trevor & Endymion Beer
ISBN 1-899383-18-2

Acknowledgements
The photographs on pages 8, 11, 19, 23, 24 and 30 are by Andrew Besley.
All other photographs are from the author's and publishers' collections.

Printed by R Booth (Troutbeck Press), Mabe, Penryn, Cornwall

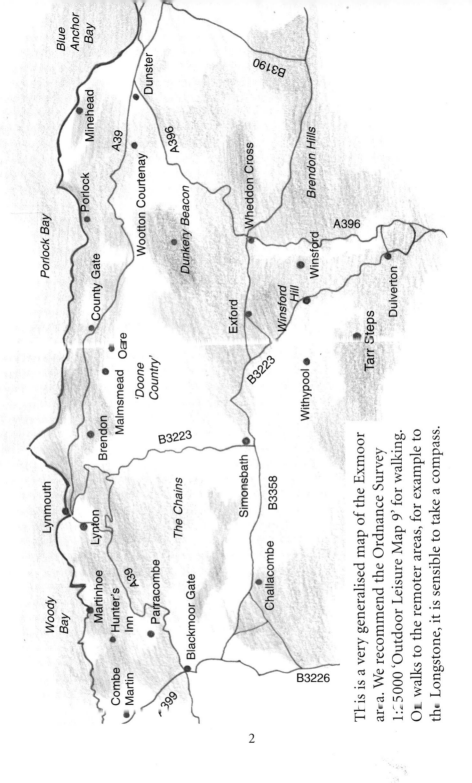

This is a very generalised map of the Exmoor area. We recommend the Ordnance Survey 1:25000 'Outdoor Leisure Map 9' for walking. On walks to the remoter areas, for example to the Longstone, it is sensible to take a compass.

A very short history

The whole of Exmoor, even the wildest parts, has long been influenced by the activities of men and women.

The Bronze Age inhabitants (c2000–c750 BC) were fairly numerous, and left many monuments, particularly barrows such as Wood Barrow near Challacombe (above). Stone does not outcrop much on Exmoor, so the stone monuments, such as menhirs, rows and circles, are fewer and less impressive than those found on Dartmoor or the Cornish moors. Nevertheless, there are still some inspiring examples to be admired.

When the climate deteriorated from around 1000 BC, the population fell dramatically and the high moorland was deserted. It was still uninhabited 2000 years later in Saxon times. Land which was unclaimed and uncultivated fell into the hands of the King. The Norman kings made the high moorland into a 'Royal Forest' – a hunting preserve, not necessarily woodland, that was governed under oppressive Forest Laws by a Warden and Foresters.

Simonsbath Lodge, now a hotel

The role of Warden was a hereditary position given to a courtier. He (or on two occasions she) could earn an income by selling the Forester's job to less exalted men, who could then make money out of rents, fines, and corruption, since they controlled all 'justice' and did not hesitate to extort by blackmail.

In 1508 the Forest area was leased out, and this 'privatisation' continued until 1819, when the Crown sold its interest to John Knight from a Midlands industrial family. At the same time, it was 'inclosed' and farmers from outside the Forest, who until then had the right to graze animals there, were bought out.

When John Knight acquired it in 1819, Exmoor Forest was quite uninhabited except for a small farm at Simonsbath. Knight and his son Frederic (who took over in 1840) built a wall 29 miles (46km) long around their estate, as well as 22 miles (35 km) of public roads connecting Simonsbath at the heart of Exmoor to the outside world, and gradually – at enormous expense – they developed a system of Exmoor agriculture which was profitable. From about 1842, they constructed farmhouses on the moor, and leased them to tenants, but it was not until around 1880 that any of these showed a profit.

The Knights established the small village at Simonsbath, and built this church in 1856

Simonsbath Lodge, now a hotel, was originally built by James Boevey, the most remarkable and notorious of the Exmoor wardens who virtually ruled over the Forest in the King's name – he eventually bought the Forest freehold. Of Dutch descent, he brought his new wife Isabel de Visscher to the Lodge in the seventeenth century, and was himself author of several odd books, including *The Art of Governing the Tongue, The Art of Gaining Wealth* and *The Act of Building a Man.*

Much of what was still wild and unenclosed land in 1800 looked by 1900 like tamed farmland, and throughout the twentieth century moorland was regularly lost to agriculture. High windbreak hedges and grass fields replaced heather and bracken.

Not all of Exmoor was included in the Forest by any means. The Forest was mainly the central, higher and uninhabited moorland. Surrounding this were small settlements consisting of a few fields and much wasteland or woodland.

In the eighteenth and nineteenth centuries, attempts were made in places to quarry minerals, especially iron ore. The fact that these industries never became hugely successful, that the sought after natural resources were not present in quantities large enough to turn the area into a major production centre, has meant Exmoor has retained its natural beauty with virtually no despoliation of the countryside. Imagine Porlock Bay as another Barrow-in-Furness, or Combe Martin and North Molton as huge mining areas!

Much of Exmoor now is a National Park of almost 300 square miles, with about one-third in Devon and two-thirds in Somerset. The National Park headquarters are at Dulverton.

Exmoor in snow. You are unlikely to meet anything like this, but do remember that weather conditions on Exmoor may change dramatically in minutes, even in summer. It is as well to be prepared, with stout footwear and sensible clothing.

Also keep an eye out for adders: they do not attack unless provoked but it is sensible to watch out for them, especially if you have a child or a dog with you

Gallox Bridge, Dunster, took packhorses across the River Avill

Dunster

Of the West Country's three great moors, Exmoor is unique in having a coastline. The moor's edge extends right to the cliffs and the little harbours along the coast were of vital importance from early times.

Dunster used to be the main town of the region, famous for its cloth industry and having an attractive octagonal Yarn Market (built in 1609) at its centre. It still retains many beautiful buildings from the middle ages including the castle, the priory, the church and the Luttrell Arms.

During Elizabeth I's reign 'Dunster Haven' was a harbour of some importance, but it silted up long ago and now Dunster Beach is renowned for its long row of chalets beloved of many generations of holidaymakers. It is a good place to relax, with lovely views of Blue Anchor Bay and the green backdrop of coastal cliffs and hills beyond. Modern tourism probably keeps the town as prosperous as it ever was, a new industry which seems to have left Dunster unspoiled.

Conygar Hill with its eighteenth century folly is an outstanding landmark. 'Conygar' possibly comes from 'Cony Garth', the old name for a rabbit warren (rabbits were known as conies).

Dunster Castle in its present form is largely a Victorian creation, although the first castle was erected just after the Norman conquest, and the Luttrell family have lived here since 1376. The castle once controlled the coast road and the strategically important route (now A396) through the hills and down the Exe Valley to Tiverton. Today owned by The National Trust, the castle is open to the public, and has many acres of parkland with thoroughbred cattle.

The octagonal Yarn Market, often called the butter market (perhaps from its use after the great days of Dunster cloth-making), was built in 1609

Minehead, showing the harbour with Beacon Hill behind

Minehead

Nearby Minehead grew as silted-up Dunster declined. Its harbour lies under Beacon Hill, with the lifeboat house just beyond and the remains of the old steamer pier, 250 yards (230 metres) long, looming out into the sea. Opened in 1901, this was demolished during World War II to improve coastal gun sightings. It was a relic of the days when the Bristol Channel was busy with paddle steamers bringing visitors to the Somerset coastal resorts. Today the *Waverley*, the last ocean-going paddle steamer in the world, and *Balmoral* moor against the harbour wall, calling at Minehead from May to October en route from Penarth and Clevedon to Ilfracombe in North Devon. Minehead itself is a jolly town to visit, with its holiday camp and funfair, and delightful countryside all around.

The restored West Somerset Railway runs regular steam

Selworthy is one of several attractive villages on the Minehead side of Porlock, and a starting point for woodland walks. The village and much of the country round about is in the care of The National Trust

trains between Bishop's Lydeard and Minehead, a twenty mile (32 km) journey via Watchet, Blue Anchor and Dunster.

In the delightful area between Minehead and Porlock, close to the sea, the climate is often so balmy that the locals say the grass grows all the year round. The fertile Vale of Porlock is renowned for its agriculture and horticulture.

Walks in the vicinity can take in Selworthy Combe, with its picturesque thatched cottages (shown above), other charming villages such as Bossington and Luccombe, some outstanding woodland, and Dunkery Beacon – at 1704 feet (519 metres) the highest hill in the National Park.

Porlock Bay and nearby Blue Anchor Bay are good bird-watching places in autumn and winter, with wintering waders and wildfowl using the area and adjacent marsh sites.

Porlock (above) and Porlock Weir (opposite)

Porlock and Porlock Weir

Porlock, like Dunster, Minehead, Wootton Courtenay and Timberscombe, lies in what is geologically known as the New Red Sandstone area of Exmoor. This contrasts with the predominant rock system of the moor, which is generally Devonian – the oldest is in the north and the youngest in the south.

In Porlock the older thatched cottages do not face on to the streets, but instead present their 'backs', a peculiar feature often remarked on by visitors. It has given rise to the phrase 'Porlock fashion' and is applied to other similarly arranged cottages elsewhere in the West Country.

The Ship Inn is where the poet Southey stayed. He wrote in his diary that Porlock was locally regarded as 'the End of the World' and that no wheeled traffic could penetrate beyond it – and if you imagine Porlock Hill as a muddy track rather than a tarmac road, it is easy to believe him.

The handsome little port of Porlock Weir is backed by a precipitous drop of almost 1400 feet (450 metres) and was always difficult of access. In the nineteenth century there was a proposal for an incline plane, rather like the cliff railway at Lynmouth, but it was never built.

Lynmouth and Lynton

'Lyn' is from the Old English 'hlynn', meaning a torrent, very appropriate for the East and West Lyn Rivers which give their name to the two towns still widely remembered for a flood tragedy of incredible summer rains in 1952 – 300 million gallons (1,400,000,000 litres) of rain fell on The Chains, a marshy watershed above Linton and Lynmouth, within five hours. The soil was already saturated with previous rainfall: the result was a heavy loss of life and devastation to property in Lynmouth.

Perhaps one of the nicest approaches to Lynmouth, if you can arrange it, is on foot from Watersmeet (park at OS map grid reference 740477) down the left bank of the river. This is an absolute joy, bringing the walker to Lynmouth and the sea. There are pleasant shops, inns and cafes here, and also the famous waterpowered Cliff Railway which plies between Lynmouth and the sister town of Lynton (where there is an interesting museum and many other facilities for visitors).

Lynmouth looking up the West Lyn Valley from the sea

The Rhenish Tower at Lynmouth

At Lynmouth the replica of a Rhenish tower on the solid stone jetty attracts great interest. Built by General Rawdon, it is an imitation of a tower on the Rhine and was intended as a beacon light for mariners and fishermen. At one time a prosperous herring fishing fleet worked out of Lynmouth, but numbers of herring around the coast have long since dwindled.

Lynton and Lynmouth are linked by a steep but well-made road and also by the Cliff Railway, an absolute must for most newcomers to see. Blasting for the route was begun in 1887 and the railway opened in 1890. The two carriages run on an endless cable and are gravity pulled. A tank in the top carriage is filled with spring water whilst the bottom carriage is emptied. When the brake is released the carriages move smoothly up and down the rails, taking about 90 seconds to complete the journey of 900 feet (275 metres). There has never been an accident on this railway in its whole history, which is a remarkable achievement of safety.

Above: The Hoar Oak Water meets the East Lyn, seen in October after heavy rainfall

Opposite: Watersmeet in early May, with the leaves not yet fully out

Watersmeet

The countryside around Watersmeet near Lynton is one of those special areas of deeply wooded coombes, sparkling waterways and peace and quiet even in the busiest times of the year. Dippers, birds of prey, salmon, trout and pleasant walking can all be enjoyed on the way down stream to Lynmouth via Myrtleberry, or up stream to Hillsford Bridge and the high country of farmland and moor, via Winston's Path.

Watersmeet (743486) is so named from the confluence of the East Lyn with the Hoar Oak Water. Close by is The National Trust tea and gift shop, once a fishing lodge built by the Hallidays of Glenthorne at County Gate on the Devon and Somerset border, but a tearoom since 1901.

Coastal scenery

Westwards from Lynton and reached via Lee Road is the ruggedly appealing Valley of Rocks and stunning coastal scenery of hog's back cliffs all the way to Woody Bay, Heddon's Mouth and beyond. The Valley can also be reached from Lynmouth along the superb North Walk, a mile-long path cut in 1817 by a Mr Sanford. From it can be seen the Welsh coast and Severn Sea, and then the delightful Valley of Rocks itself with Castle Rock, Ragged Jack and the Devil's Cheesewring.

The valley is unique in England in running parallel with the sea, not inland from it, due to the rivers cutting deeply during the last Ice Age. Now totally dry, its extraordinary landscape features are home to a herd of wild goats.

The famous 'Mother Meldrum's Kitchen' is found here too. Mother Meldrum was the old soothsayer and wise woman of R D Blackmore's *Lorna Doone*. Her 'Kitchen' is situated in the

Mother Meldrum's Kitchen in the Valley of Rocks

Cheesewring area and is signposted. Amongst rock clitter just left of the signed Cheesewring Path is an ancient stone circle once believed to have Druid connections. Still vaguely visible, unfortunately it has been vandalised and needs restoring.

Continuing westward along the coast path from the valley, within the Lee Abbey Estate, the Duty Point tower stands on the cliff edge. Lovers of great English landscape paintings will be interested to know this is 'The Lonely Tower' of Samuel Palmer's wonderful paintings. He visited the area around 1835. Lee Abbey is a farmed estate run by a Christian community, and has holiday accommodation.

The road west from the Valley of Rocks takes you to Woody Bay via the estate Toll Road. Woody Bay, with its steep-hanging oak woods rising to over 900 feet (275 metres), has a hotel open to non-residents and there is an excellent 'cream tea' cottage just by the Lee Abbey Toll-Gate. Indeed the breathtaking coast path walk from here to Hunter's Inn brings you to further refreshments and another well situated National Trust Shop which prides itself on its ice-creams, so it's a great area for treats!

Woody Bay to Heddon's Mouth via the lower coast path for the waterfall cascade and seabirds is one of the best coastal walks on Exmoor: there are razorbills, guillemots and fulmars, and photographic opportunities galore.

Hunter's Inn can also be reached by a road which then becomes a well maintained track to Heddon's Mouth along the Heddon River Valley, reputedly the warmest valley in England. There is a newly restored lime kiln here by the sea, along with awe-inspiring scenery, soaring buzzards and purple heather-clad slopes come August time.

West of Heddon's Mouth (655497) the coast path leads to Combe Martin, settled in its attractive seaside surroundings close to the Hangman Hills. This pretty village with its famous long main street to the sea and its history of horticulture, including the nurturing of delicious strawberries, is the last point of the Exmoor National Park boundary.

Woody Bay

The Longstone (705431) is an impressive standing stone, 9 feet (nearly 3 metres) tall and made of slate, so that it is very thin if looked at from the side. It is said by some to be a fertility menhir and is on an important ley line or earth energy route. It is often visited for healing purposes

Antiquities

There are many barrows, stone circles and other antiquities on Exmoor that are worth a visit. The photograph on page 3 shows Wood Barrow (716425) which can be reached in a circular walk which takes in Wood Barrow from Breakneck Hole car park and Pinkery Pond via Pinkery Farm.

Chapman Barrows (696436), eleven in all, eight of them on the boundary between the parishes of Challacombe and Parracombe, suggest quite a population lived hereabouts in the Bronze Age. Reached along the lane to Withecombe Farm and the track beyond, Chapman Barrows is superbly sited with the whole of Exmoor lying eastwards, and Dartmoor showing to the south.

Another good area to take in is Withypool Common, where the moorland scenery capped by Brightworthy Barrows

The stone circle on Withypool Hill

(817351) is splendid. The adjoining Withypool Hill is the site of an archaeologically superb stone circle (838343), as well as a barrow, but don't expect a Stonehenge lookalike!

The Caratacus Stone (890335) dates from about the sixth century AD, inscribed 'Cara(t)aci nepos'. 'Carataci' means 'of Caractacus', but 'nepos' can be translated as grandchild, nephew or descendant. Probably a local chief was boosting his prestige by claiming to be a descendant of the great British warrior.

Tarr Steps (868322) near Dulverton is in delightful farming countryside. Passing over the River Barle, this bridge or causeway that is said by some to be prehistoric and by others to be medieval is without doubt the finest of its type in England. It has 17 spans of flat stone slabs supported on stone piers laid on the river bed. One of the larger slabs weighs about two tonnes. Sloping stones angled against the piers (see photograph) protect the structure from the rushing current. Including the paved approach, the bridge is about 180 feet (55 metres) in length and stands around 3 feet (1 metre) above the water surface. All but one span was swept away during the 1952 floods which devastated the Lynton and Lynmouth area. The bridge was later restored by Somerset County Council. Various beings have been associated with the building of Tarr Steps including fairies, giants, Nordic gods and Old Nick himself, who is said to sunbathe here. Tarr Steps Farm serves refreshments.

The Barle is the largest river in the region even though it is the Exe that gives its name to Exmoor. The Barle rises in The Chains and eventually joins the Exe below Dulverton on Exmoor's southern boundary.

Below Tarr Steps at the foot of Hawkridge is the confluence of the Danes Brook with the Barle, a wildly beautiful spot with the wooded slopes of the ridge towering up to the bare summit. The lovely church of St Giles, Hawkridge (861307), has a fine Norman door and font.

This area is 'Beast of Exmoor' country, with sightings of mysterious big cats reported from here and along the Exe, which meets up with the Barle some 2 miles (3 km) from Dulverton.

Tarr Steps may be prehistoric or perhaps medieval

Red deer

Exmoor, with the Scottish Highlands, is the last secure haunt of the wild red deer. They are the largest of Britain's wild mammals, holding to a stable population despite much poaching for venison and heads.

The true red of the deer's summer coat looks quite splendid, but a thicker, darker coat is grown for the winter. This is impenetrable by the worst of Exmoor's storms and bitter cold.

The stags drop their antlers annually in April, though shedding may be delayed in a cold late spring, and then the process will occur in May. When new growth begins to appear, a tissue of blood vessels covers the growing horn and feeds it. The stag is said to be 'in velvet' at this time. By late August or early September the antlers are fully renewed, the velvet having dried up. An adult stag goes through this remarkable process for four months every year of its life.

The main rut lasts three to four weeks, starting in late September. Larger stags round up as many hinds as they can hold and then defend them against other stags.The female red deer, the hinds, are ready to mate in their second year, and they generally produce one calf, usually in June. The gestation period is eight months. Calves are leggy, dappled creatures for the first three or four months of their lives after which their coats become unspotted and red like the adults.

Most active at dawn and dusk, red deer live in a range of habitats, but they are basically woodland animals, emerging from tree cover to feed in adjacent fields in the evenings.

Grasses, sedges and rushes are their most important food throughout the year, but heather and small shrubs, ferns, mushrooms, herbs, lichens and tree bark also feature in their diet. Holly is often a popular food in hard winters when there is snow on the ground.

Adult red deer have no natural predators except man, and there is ongoing controversy as to whether there is a need to cull them.

A mixed group of stags and hinds. The stags are 'in velvet' with their new antlers partly grown

Exmoor ponies

The Exmoor pony is indigenous to the area. It is a wild species directly descended from the prehistoric wild horse and it is one of the hardiest of British wild animals. The ponies' true colour is brown, ranging from a smoky hue to a reddish one. The underparts, muzzle and insides of the legs are mealy, or fawn, coloured, while the mane and tail are black.

The lighter coloured foals are born in June, their coats darkening as they grow and gleaming in the summer months. They then thicken in winter to form as watertight a covering as the red deer has.

Herds roam the moor all year round, comprising thirty or forty mares and foals and a stallion as leader. Cross-breeding diminishes the ponies' hardiness and only the true Exmoors survive the worst of the winters such as those of 1947, 1962 and 1963 which decimated much of Exmoor's wildlife.

The Exmoor Pony Society, founded in 1920, has done sterling work to maintain the purity of the breed and prevent it from dying out. Cross-breeds, caused by a variety of 'non-Exmoors' being turned out for grazing, are still known as 'Porlock ponies' in some parts.

The wild Exmoor ponies belong to the owner of the land they stand on. The old tradition of an annual round-up still continues, with many being sold at Bampton Fair in October. The remainder are freed once more to rove the moors: Withypool Common and Hill have the finest herds of these appealing animals.

The indigenous Exmoor pony evolved to withstand harsh winter conditions. Cross-breeds are generally less hardy

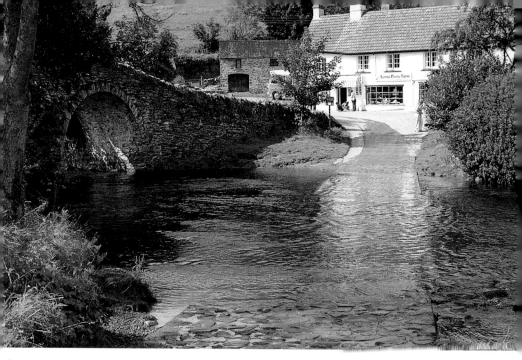

Malmsmead, heart of Lorna Doone Country

Doone Country

Two novels – Henry Williamson's *Tarka the Otter* and RD
Blackmore's *Lorna Doone* – are hard to avoid around Exmoor,
especially as the tourist authorities use them to promote the
area. Both books became best-sellers because of their passionate
descriptions of nature, but both authors resented being known
mainly for one work: each thought he had written better mate-
rial elsewhere!

The story of a band of outlawed Scottish gentry – the notorious Doones – was current before Blackmore's time, as was the
story of Tom Faggus, the highwayman referred to in the tale.
His long-gun is still to be seen at the Museum of North Devon
at Barnstaple.

Malmsmead (793477) is in the heart of Lorna Doone country and the place from which to explore. There is good walking
along the lovely Badgworthy ('Badgery') Water, which forms

the boundary between Devon and Somerset. You can leave your car in the Exmoor National Park Authority car park and/or take advantage of the pony riding facilities and 'Lorna Doone Farm' teas and gift shop. The attractive bridge and ford must be one of the most photographed places on Exmoor.

The Exmoor Natural History Society's Field Centre is just over the bridge and up the road from Lorna Doone Farm. A programme of guided walks is generally available during spring and summer.

Blackmore's memorial stone is along the path from Malmsmead to the Doone Valley. Malmsmead was once known as Moles Mead and, with Lorna Doone Farm, was the gateway to the Doone country. It was formerly the home of the Snow family until they acquired Oare Manor House through marriage in the eighteenth century. Oare House was the site of the Plover's Barrow Farm referred to by Blackmore.

Mounds beside the track at the eastern approach to Holcombe Coombe from Badgworthy Water are all that remains of

Ancient beeches near an old farm ruin, with Swincombe and Challacombe beyond

Badgworthy ('Badgery') Water – the most renowned of Exmoor's smaller rivers, it merges with Oare Water to become the East Lyn

a ruined settlement, the 'cots' of the Doones from the story. These were deserted by 1400, though Blackmore's Doones lived in the 17th century. The shepherd's cottage to the west is much later. The 'waterslide' is thought to be the one that runs down the valley side of Lank Combe. Oare Church (803473) is extremely popular, for it is here, according to the Doone Legend, that Lorna was shot by Carver on her wedding day. She lived on of course, as does the great romance based on Exmoor, drawing many thousands of visitors to the area each year.

The walking is easy, the paths good enough. Where the route goes westwards to high open moorland the track is indistinct: it's easy to follow in good weather but in misty conditions it is wise to have a compass handy and know how to use it.

There are magnificent views from the elevated points, so a clear day is best for appreciating the true splendour of the land-scape with its abundance of wildlife species including dippers, buzzards and many wildflowers.

Above: the wilds of 'Doone Country'

Right: Oare Church, where in the Doone legend Carver Doone shot Lorna on her wedding day

Where to walk

Here are three suggested short walks using OS map 9, 'Exmoor', from the Outdoor Leisure Map series. The map carries an explanation of how to use the grid references. All starting points are near a car park.

1. *Minehead's North Hill.* Start Martlet Hill, 969463. An easy 3-mile (5 km) walk. Follow track to 962469, and take a stony track past old wartime marshalling area and along a ridge with views of Dunkery and the Welsh coast. Above Burgundy Chapel Combe, 947476, turn right and follow official SW Coast Path back to Minehead.

2. *Horner, Luccombe, Woodcock Gardens, Webbers Post and back to Horner.* 4 miles (6 km) undulating through trees and over moorland. Start 898454 along lane to Luccombe and pass Horner Mill, turning right onto steep track and straight on SE to Chapel Cross, Luccombe Church. Follow waymarked route along Stoney Lane (now tarmac) to Woodcock Gardens, taking the first turn shown on the map up between Woodcock and Yonder Gardens. Follow Dunster Path up to Webber's Post car park. Superb views. Go N following a gently descending hill and then a final steep drop to Horner Mill with tea gardens and car park start point nearby.

3. *Dulverton, Burridge Wood, Kennel Farm, Marsh Bridge, Looseall Wood, Court Down and back to Dulverton.* 4 miles (6 km). Park beside Exmoor National Park HQ, 913278. Short walk through woods and meadows, with one hill to ascend. Cross the bridge and turn right into lane, and right again along a footpath which climbs up, then down to the valley bottom. Waymarked route – 'ENPA'.

If you don't wish to move far from your vehicle, these car parks offer seating and fine views of the surrounding countryside and coast:

Dunster Castle car park near Gallox Bridge, grid reference 990433
Exmoor National Park car park, Malmsmead, 793477
Webber's Post car park, 903438
National Trust car park, Horner Valley, 897455
Selworthy Church car park, 920467
Watersmeet car park, 740477
National Trust car park, Countisbury, 747496
National Trust car park, Woody Bay, 676486
Badlake Moor Cross, 857284